GCSE Music
Revision Guide

Alan Charlton

RHINEGOLD
EDUCATION

www.rhinegoldeducation.co.uk

Music Study Guides

GCSE, AS and A2 Music Study Guides (AQA, Edexcel and OCR)
GCSE, AS and A2 Music Listening Tests (AQA, Edexcel and OCR)
GCSE, AS and A2 Music Revison Guides (AQA, Edexcel and OCR)
AS/A2 Music Technology Study Guide (Edexcel)
AS/A2 Music Technology Listening Tests (Edexcel)
AS and A2 Music Technology Revision Guides (Edexcel)

Also available from Rhinegold Education

AS and A2 Music Harmony Workbooks
GCSE and AS Music Composition Workbooks
GCSE and AS Music Literacy Workbooks
Romanticism in Focus, Baroque Music in Focus, Modernism in Focus, Film Music in Focus,
Musicals in Focus
Music Technology from Scratch

First published 2010 in Great Britain by
Rhinegold Education
14–15 Berners Street
London W1T 3LJ

www.rhinegoldeducation.co.uk

© Rhinegold Education 2010
a division of Music Sales Limited

You should always check the current requirements of the examination, since these may change.
Copies of the AQA specification can be downloaded from the AQA website at www.aqa.org.uk
AQA Publications (queries only) telephone: 0844 209 6614, fax: 0161 836 4545, email: publications@aqa.org.uk

AQA GCSE Music Revision Guide
Order No. RHG331
ISBN: 978-1-907447-16-7

Exclusive Distributors:
Music Sales Ltd
Distribution Centre, Newmarket Road
Bury St Edmunds, Suffolk IP33 3YB, UK

Printed in the EU

Contents

The author

Alan Charlton is a composer, writer, examiner and teacher. He holds a PhD in Composition from Bristol University and was the first Eileen Norris Fellow in Composition at Bedford School. A winner of many national and international awards for composition, performers of his music include The Lindsays and Birmingham Contemporary Music Group. He was Head of Music Technology at Bedford School for four years and is also an experienced Edexcel examiner and teacher of GCSE and A-level music. He has written and contributed to many books and study guides on music and has written for *Classroom Music* magazine.

Acknowledgements

The author would like to thank the consultant Paul Terry and the Rhinegold Education editorial and design team of Harriet Power and Reema Patel for their expert support in the preparation of this book.

Introduction

This guide is intended to help you prepare for your AQA GCSE Listening to and Appraising Music exam (Unit 1) which you take at the end of your AQA GCSE Music course. Before you begin, do make sure that you are actually following the **AQA** specification and not OCR or Edexcel.

In this guide there are helpful **revision tips**, sections on each of the topics in the three AQA **strands**, a revision of the **elements of music** and a **glossary** of musical terms used in the book. It is best to start by planning your revision using the revision tips before moving on to the rest of the book.

The one-hour exam will include a number of **short extracts of recorded music** from the topics you have studied, with several questions on each. The sample paper provided by AQA suggests that there could be at least 12 extracts, most of which are unlikely to be much longer than 30 seconds, and each of which will be played several times. Most questions can be answered in a single word or short phrase, but a few may require slightly longer answers.

Although the extracts will all be related to the topics you have covered, they are unlikely to come from the precise works you studied on the course. For that reason, the pieces suggested for listening in the second half of this book (from page 24 onwards) have been chosen to broaden your knowledge of the topics concerned and to help you practise listening to unfamiliar music. However, remember that in the exam the extracts will mostly be very short and the questions on them will focus on the use of the **elements of music**, such as melody, tonality, texture and so on – you will not be asked to give precise dates of composition or details about specific composers.

Therefore, **concentrate on revising the elements of music**. There are short questions throughout this guide to help you with your revision: **answers** to these may be found at www.rhinegoldeducation.co.uk. On this website you can also find a link to a **Spotify playlist** to accompany the musical examples in this guide. Listen to each of these tracks with the corresponding section of the guide, making sure that you understand the points made about them.

Finally, try to combine this guide with some practice listening tests. This will put the information you are learning from this guide into context. There are more details on getting hold of practice papers in the revision tips section.

Good luck!

Top ten revision tips

1. PLAN YOUR REVISION

Start revising as soon as you can, using the Christmas and Easter holidays if possible. The earlier you can start preparing, the happier and more confident you will be in the weeks leading up to the exam.

First **devise a rough, overall plan**, deciding how much time you're going to spend on GCSE Music and, within that, how much time you're going to allocate to each topic. The most effective approach is to tackle the topics you are **least confident** about first, leaving your strengths until last. Include 'rest days' to avoid becoming jaded, and some 'general revision days' to give yourself some extra time if you need to catch up or cover a topic in more detail.

EXAMPLE 1

Time left: 15 days. Need to cover 18 topics. Two topics per day = 9 days, plus 2 rest days, plus 4 days of general revision.

- ■ Monday: rhythm and metre, and music for voices
- ■ Tuesday: chamber music and music of Africa
- ■ Wednesday: film music, and timbre and dynamics
- ■ Etc.

EXAMPLE 2

Time left: 30 days. Need to cover 18 topics. One topic per day = 18 days, plus 4 rest days, plus 8 days of general revision.

- ■ Monday: music theatre
- ■ Tuesday: harmony and tonality
- ■ Wednesday: music of India
- ■ Etc.

Ideally, draw up detailed plans of each day. People tend to revise most effectively in short concentrated bursts of about 20 minutes to half an hour, so structure your revision around sessions of this length, giving yourself plenty of breaks in which to switch off. Start each revision session by reminding and testing yourself on what you learnt in the previous session. Don't be too ambitious about what you can achieve in a day as you will soon get behind: 6–8 hours of revision (including short breaks) is a realistic maximum.

EXAMPLE 3

Wednesday:

9.00–9.20	Go through the 'test yourself' questions on Tuesday's topics, writing out the answers
9.20–9.30	Break
9.30–9.50	The concerto: revise context and key features
9.50–10.00	Break
10.00–10.30	The concerto: suggested listening and test yourself questions
10.30–10.45	Break
10.45–11.05	Music theatre: revise background and key features
11.05–11.15	Break
11.15–11.45	Music theatre: suggested listening and test yourself questions
11.45–12.00	Break

Once you have a plan, do your best to stick to it, otherwise you will need to spend more time devising another plan.

2. PRACTISE YOUR LISTENING SKILLS

Remember that as you are revising for a listening exam, the most important thing to do is to practise your listening skills, which means **listening to music and trying to describe it** using the correct musical terminology. So for each topic, listen to the suggested listening and go through the features to listen out for, making sure you can hear them in the music. Check that you have absorbed this by listening again without this guide, writing down as many points as you can remember.

3. USE THE PLAYLIST

If you are able to, download the **Spotify playlist** that accompanies this revision guide from www.rhinegoldeducation.co.uk, which contains all of the suggested listening given for each topic. You can then listen to this in 'shuffle' mode in your spare time, familiarising yourself with the sounds of the different genres you need to learn. If you are unable to do this, your teacher may be able to help by lending you their own listening materials.

4. CARRY OUT YOUR OWN RESEARCH

You are much more likely to remember things that you have **found out for yourself**. Try looking through books in your school or local library, or use websites such as Wikipedia,

Spotify, the BBC website, YouTube and Google. It's much easier to remember an artist's name or identify an instrument if you've seen a photo or video of them.

5. KEEP A NOTEBOOK

Every time you come across a word you don't recognise or have forgotten, look it up in the glossary and **write out the word and its meaning** in the notebook. Read through and test yourself regularly on these words until you have learned them by heart, and make sure you can identify the **sound** to which each musical term refers.

6. USE PRACTICE PAPERS

Ask your teacher if they can give you some **practice papers**. When completing these, try to do so in exam conditions. If they have time, ask your teacher if they can mark them and help you with any questions you were unsure about. Then have another go at these questions to give you confidence if anything similar appears in your exam. If your teacher doesn't have time, they may be able to give you a mark scheme, or you may be able to access this on your exam board's website.

The *AQA GCSE Music Listening Tests* from Rhinegold Education includes over 30 practice listening questions, as well as general advice to help you develop your listening skills.

7. REVISE IN A QUIET, DISTRACTION-FREE PLACE

Unless you are using them for revision, **avoid distractions** such as the internet, background music and your mobile. Consider revising in your local library, where it is much harder to get distracted.

8. ANALYSE EVERYTHING YOU HEAR

Practise developing your listening skills by **analysing any music you hear**: music on the radio, background music to TV programmes, adverts and so on. What textures does it use? Is it major or minor? What is its time signature and tempo? Which instruments are playing? How would you describe the style of the music? What is its purpose? When and where was it written? Every so often, switch on Radio 1, 2 or 3 to give yourself some extra listening practice. There are usually schedules on the BBC website, so you can check what you are listening to and google the title, artist or composer to find out more about them.

9. USE YOUR OWN INSTRUMENTAL KNOWLEDGE

Try to **make connections between what you are learning and music you have played** or know well. For instance, when you are revising terms such as syncopation, riff or conjunct movement, try to think if there are any examples of these from pieces you know well. You could also take a piece you have recently played and try to describe it as accurately as you can using musical terminology.

10. FOCUS ON THE ELEMENTS OF MUSIC

If time is short, **focus on the elements of music and musical features of each topic**, as most exam questions will be testing you on musical terminology rather than historical facts. With questions on notation (filling in the missing pitches or rhythms), if you are not very confident about reading staff notation and have little time to revise for the exam, your time may be better used preparing for other aspects of the exam. If, however, you are confident, it is worth spending some time practising dictation tests. Your music teacher or an instrumental teacher may be able to help you with these.

The elements of music

The main key to success in the listening exam is being able to comment on how the elements of music are used in the extracts you are played. AQA splits the 'elements' into the following:

1. Rhythm and metre
2. Harmony and tonality
3. Texture and melody
4. Timbre and dynamics
5. Structure and form.

It is very important to try to understand the concepts in this section as fully as you can. This knowledge is not only helpful for answering direct listening questions on pitch, rhythm, instrumentation and so on, but it will also make questions on topics such as the concerto or music theatre much easier to answer.

Make sure you can recognise these elements **by ear** – try to find them in a piece of music you can play, or in a CD you own.

This chapter gives you a brief reminder of all of the terms you are expected to know for your written exam. If you have any difficulty in understanding them, go to the Rhinegold Education *AQA GCSE Music Study Guide* for a more thorough explanation. The Rhinegold Education *GCSE Music Literacy Workbook* might also be very useful if you don't feel particularly confident about the areas covered in this chapter.

RHYTHM AND METRE

Questions on rhythm and metre may ask you to notate a rhythm, identify a time signature, or describe the rhythm and tempo of a passage of music.

BASIC TERMS

■ **Pulse** or **metre**: the **beat** of the music. Most music has a **regular** pulse/metre.
■ **Tempo**: the **speed** of the music. This is usually indicated in **beats per minute** (e.g. 60 bpm) or as a **metronome mark** (e.g. $\downarrow$ = 60), or by terms such as 'Allegro' (fast).
■ **Time signature**: indicates the number of **beats** in a bar. Time signatures can be divided into **two** main categories:
　1. **Simple time**: the beat subdivides into **two**. E.g. in $\frac{2}{4}$ the pulse consists of two crotchets, each of which subdivides into two quavers. Common metres in simple time are: $\frac{2}{4}$, $\frac{4}{4}$ and $\frac{2}{2}$.
　2. **Compound time**: the beat subdivides into **three**. E.g. in $\frac{6}{8}$ the pulse consists of two dotted crotchets, each of which subdivides into three quavers. Common metres in compound time are: $\frac{6}{8}$, $\frac{9}{8}$ and $\frac{12}{8}$.

NOTE LENGTHS

Note	Rest	Name	Number of crotchet beats
𝅝	▬	Semibreve	4
𝅗𝅥.	▬·	Dotted minim	3
𝅗𝅥	▬	Minim	2
♩.	𝄽·	Dotted crotchet	1½
♩	𝄽	Crotchet	1
♪	𝄾	Quaver	½
𝅘𝅥𝅯	𝄿	Semiquaver	¼

CHARACTERISTIC RHYTHMIC PATTERNS

- **Dotted rhythms**: these are made up of **pairs of notes** in the pattern **long–short**. The first note is **dotted** and the second is one **third** of the dotted note's value.
- **Triplets**: a triplet is created when **three** notes are fitted into the time of **two**.
- **Syncopation**: this occurs when weak beats or off-beats are **accented**. Look out for syncopation in jazz and popular music in particular.
- **Augmentation**: a rhythm is repeated in a **longer** version, often with note values **doubled**.
- **Diminution**: a rhythm is repeated in a **shorter** version, often with note values **halved**.
- **Cross rhythm**: created when two **conflicting rhythms** occur at the same time.
- **Hemiola**: a type of cross rhythm where **two** bars of $\frac{3}{4}$ sound like **three** bars of $\frac{2}{4}$. This is commonly found in Baroque music, in the two bars before the final chord of a cadence.

OTHER RHYTHMIC EFFECTS

- **Polyrhythm**: more than two **conflicting rhythms** are heard at the same time.
- **Irregular metres**: frequent **changes** of time signature occur, preventing a regular sense of pulse from being established.
- **Free time**: the performer interprets the rhythm **without a regular beat**.
- **Rubato**: a strictly notated rhythm is played with a degree of **flexibility**, as long as a basic sense of pulse in maintained. Rubato is often used in Romantic music.

HARMONY

'Harmony' means anything to do with chords and chord progressions. Questions on harmony may ask you to name a cadence, spot a special harmonic feature or describe the chords used in a passage of music.

BASIC TERMS

- **Consonant**: describes notes that sound **pleasing** together
- **Dissonant**: describes notes that seem to **clash** with each other
- **Diatonic**: the music uses only the notes of the current key
- **Chromatic**: the music contains notes that don't belong to the key the music is currently in.

CHORDS

A **triad** is a chord with **three notes**, with each note separated by an interval of a **3rd**. You can build a triad on each note of a major or minor scale. The chords that result are referred to by **Roman numerals**.

- A **lowercase** numeral (e.g. ii) means that the chord is **minor**
- An **uppercase** numeral (e.g. IV) means that the chord is **major**.

Each note in the scale is also given a **name**, such as tonic, mediant or dominant.

Here are the major and minor **triads** on each note of the C major scale, together with their **chord symbols** and **Roman numerals**:

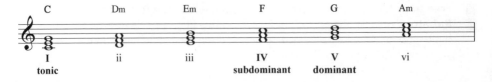

The most important chords to remember in any key are the **tonic** (I), **subdominant** (IV) and **dominant** (V).

One other chord that you should be able to recognise is the **dominant 7th**. This is a **triad** on the **dominant** (V), with an **extra note** a **7th** above the tonic. E.g. in C major, the dominant 7th chord contains the notes G–B–D–F.

CADENCES

A **cadence** is the term for a short chord progression that is used to end a musical phrase. There are four different types:

1. **Perfect**: V–I (sounds strong and final)
2. **Imperfect**: ends on chord V, e.g. I–V or ii–V (sounds incomplete)
3. **Plagal**: IV–I (often used to sing 'Amen' to in church music)
4. **Interrupted**: V–VI (sounds like a surprise).

Sometimes a piece in a minor key will end with a **major** tonic chord, rather than a minor one. This is called a **tierce de Picardie**.

OTHER HARMONIC FEATURES

- **Pedal note** or **drone**: a note that is **held** or **repeated** (usually in the **bass**), while the harmonies above it change.

TEST YOURSELF

1. What is the difference between music that is consonant and music that is dissonant?
2. Which notes make up a dominant 7th chord in the key of D major?
3. In the key of A minor, which two chords create a perfect cadence?

TONALITY

'Tonality' refers to keys. If you are asked a question on tonality, you might be expected to say whether a passage of music is minor or major, or to describe any modulations that occur.

BASIC TERMS

- **Tonal**: in a **major** or **minor** key
- **Atonal**: not in any key
- **Modal**: based on a type of seven-note scale called a 'mode'.

KEY SIGNATURES

The **key** of a piece of music indicates which scale it is based on. For example, music in the key of D major uses notes of the D major scale.

Each key has its own **key signature**. This shows which notes on the stave are to be played as sharps or flats.

These are the key signatures you will be expected to recognise for GCSE:

Sharps:

C major *or*	G major *or*	D major *or*	A major *or*	E major *or*
A minor	E minor	B minor	F♯ minor	C♯ minor

Flats:

F major *or*	B♭ major *or*	E♭ major *or*	A♭ major *or*
D minor	G minor	C minor	F minor

MODULATION

Modulation is the process of moving from one key to another. It usually happens in **three** stages:

1. The initial key is established
2. The music reaches a chord that is common to both keys (called a **pivot chord**)
3. The music continues in the new key, usually confirming it with a cadence.

Common modulations are to:

- The **dominant** (V)
- The **subdominant** (IV)
- The **relative major** or **relative minor**. The relative major of a minor key has the **same key signature** as that minor key (e.g. D major is the relative major of B minor). Likewise, the relative minor of a major key shares the same key signature as that major key (e.g. A minor is the relative minor of C major).

TEST YOURSELF

1. What is the difference between music that is modal and music that's atonal?
2. How many sharps does the key signature of A major have?
3. What is the relative major of D minor?

TEXTURE

Texture refers to the different lines or layers in a piece of music – how many there are and how they interact with each other. Questions on texture will either ask you to name a type of texture (such as homophonic), or to give a more detailed description in which you also describe how the parts played by different instruments are related to each other.

Aim to use one or more of the terms below when answering questions on texture:

- **Single melody line**: an unaccompanied melody.
- **Homophonic**: a texture consisting of an accompanied melody, often described as chordal (or harmonic) if the accompaniment moves mainly in the same rhythm as the melody.
- **Contrapuntal/polyphonic**: a texture made up of two or more melodies, heard at the same time. Each melodic line is of more-or-less equal importance.
- **Melody and accompaniment**: a melody line (usually at the top of the texture) with accompaniment.
- **Imitative**: the opening of a melody is **copied** in one or more other parts in the texture, while the original melody continues. The copied versions may be at the same or different pitches to the original.
- **Canonic**: an imitative texture in which the copied versions of the melody are **identical** to the original.
- **Layered**: a texture consisting of several different ideas superimposed on top of each other (like the layers in a cake).
- **Antiphonal**: two instrumental or vocal groups alternate with each other in a musical conversation.
- **Octaves**: the melody line is doubled in one or more different octaves.
- **Unison**: everyone performs the same note or melody.

TEST YOURSELF

1. Which of the following terms describes a texture in which there are two or more independent melodies?
   (a) contrapuntal   (b) homophonic   (c) imitative
2. What is the difference between a unison melody, and one in octaves?
3. What term is used for a texture in which the performers are split into two groups?

Questions on melody might ask you to complete the missing pitches in a short melody, identify an interval, describe the contour of a melody or name a particular ornament or melodic device.

INTERVALS

An **interval** is the distance between two different notes. Revise the intervals below, and try to make sure you can identify them by ear:

SCALES

Nearly every piece of music is based on a particular type of scale. The following terms will help you show how the notes of a melody are related to different scales:

- **Diatonic**: based entirely on notes of the current key.
- **Chromatic**: the music contains notes that don't belong to the current key of the music.
- **Pentatonic**: a scale made up of only **five notes** (e.g. C–D–E–G–A).
- **Whole tone**: a **six-note scale** in which there is an interval of a **tone** between each note (e.g. C–D–E–F♯–G♯–A♯).
- **Blues scale**: a major scale with flattened third, fifth and seventh degrees (e.g. C–E♭–F–G♭–G♮–B♭). The flattened notes are called **blue notes**.
- **Modal**: based on a type of seven-note scale (which isn't major or minor) called a 'mode'. There are different types of modes, each with set interval patterns. One example is the Dorian mode, which (starting on D) uses the notes D–E–F–G–A–B–C–D.

MELODIC CONTOUR

If asked to describe the **shape** or **contour** of a melody, possible terms to consider include:

- **Conjunct**: movement mostly by **step**
- **Disjunct**: movement in larger intervals (by **leap**)
- **Ascending**: the melody **rises**
- **Descending**: the melody **descends**
- **Triadic**: centred around the notes of one or more **triads**

- **Scalic**: uses scale patterns
- Based on **arpeggios** or **broken chords**: the notes of a chord are heard one after the other rather than at the same time.

ORNAMENTATION

Ornaments are extra notes that are added to **decorate** a melody. The ones you will need to know are:

- **Passing note**: a note that isn't part of the current chord and that comes between two notes a 3rd apart
- **Appoggiatura**: a dissonant note that is usually approached by a **leap**, and then moves by **step** to resolve on to a harmony note
- **Acciaccatura**: a quick note that precedes the main note
- **Glissando/portamento/slide**: a smooth **slide** between two notes, usually more than a semitone apart
- **Pitch bend**: a **short slide** up or down to a main note.

DEVELOPING MELODIES

The following techniques might be used to repeat or develop a melody:

- **Ostinato**: a short melodic idea that is **repeated** continually (called a **riff** in popular music)
- **Sequence**: a melodic idea (usually of one or two bars) that is immediately **repeated** at a **different pitch**
- **Inversion**: a melodic idea that has been turned **upside-down**. Every upwards step or leap is changed to a downwards one, and vice versa.

TEST YOURSELF

1. Name the following intervals (the lowest note is first):
   (a) C–F   (b) E–G♯   (c) D–C   (d) G–E♭
2. In a blues scale, which **three** notes are often flattened?
3. What is the difference between an appoggiatura and an acciaccatura?
4. What are the **two** terms you can use to describe a short melodic idea that is repeated many times?

DYNAMICS

'Dynamic' is another word for volume – how loud or quiet the music is. Questions on dynamics may ask you to explain what is meant by a certain dynamic marking or symbol, or to describe the dynamics in a passage of music.

Symbol	Italian term	Meaning
pp	pianissimo	very soft
p	piano	soft
mp	mezzo piano	quite quiet
mf	mezzo forte	quite loud
f	forte	loud
ff	fortissimo	very loud
sfz	sforzando	strong attack to a note
<	crescendo	gradually get louder
>	diminuendo	gradually get softer

TEST YOURSELF

1. What does the dynamic marking *pp* mean?
2. What is the difference between a sforzando and a crescendo?
3. Which is louder, *mp* or *mf*?

STRUCTURE AND FORM

The 'structure' or 'form' of a piece describes its overall shape – how many sections there are, and whether they repeat or differ. You might be expected to spot the following structures in your exam.

CLASSICAL MUSIC FORMS

Binary: | A | B | (Each of these sections is normally repeated, i.e. AABB)

Ternary: | A | B | A |

Rondo: | A | B | A | C | A |

Theme and variations:

Theme	Variation 1	Variation 2	Variation 3	Variation 4

The variations are based on the theme and can differ in texture, melody, harmony, rhythm and tempo, or any combination of these.

Sonata form:

Exposition		Development	Recapitulation	
1st subject (tonic)	2nd subject (dominant/ relative major)	(various keys)	1st subject (tonic)	2nd subject (tonic)

Often used for the **first movement** of a work such as a symphony or concerto.

Minuet and trio:

Minuet	Trio	Minuet

The minuet is an **elegant dance** in $\frac{3}{4}$, with a **moderate tempo**. It is often contrasted with a trio, and used for the **third movement** of a work such as a symphony.

Scherzo and trio:

Scherzo	Trio	Scherzo

Scherzo is Italian for 'joke', and the scherzo is a **lively dance** in $\frac{3}{4}$ with a **fast tempo**. Like the minuet, it is often combined with a trio and used for the **third movement** of a work.

Ground bass:

Other ideas, which evolve as the piece progresses							
Ground bass	Ground bass	Ground bass	Ground bass	Ground bass	Ground bass	Ground bass	Ground bass

A piece where the **bass line** is a **repeated phrase**. It was popular in the **Baroque period**.

Strophic:

Verse 1	Verse 2 (different words, same music)	Verse 3 (different words, same music)

In a song, the same music is used for each verse of lyrics, like in a hymn.

Through-composed:

Verse 1	Verse 2 (different music)	Verse 3 (different music)

In a song, different music is used for each verse of lyrics.

Da capo aria:

A	B	A

A piece for a **solo singer** with an **instrumental accompaniment**. Only the first two sections are written out by the composer, and the instruction '**da capo**' at the end of section B informs the singer they need to return to the beginning to repeat section A. This repeat of A is usually **decorated** by the singer. The da capo aria was popular in the **Baroque period**.

POPULAR MUSIC FORMS

Call and response:

Call	Response	Call	Response	Call	Response

One part sings a phrase (the **call**), and another part responds with an answering phrase (the **response**). This usually occurs between a soloist and a larger group.

32-bar song form:

A	A	B	A

Called 32-bar song form because each phrase often lasts for 8 bars. This structure is popular for the choruses of songs in **musicals**.

Verse-chorus form:

Intro	Verse 1	Chorus	Verse 2	Chorus	Bridge	Chorus	Outro

In its most simple version, verse-chorus form just alternates **verses** and **choruses**. There is usually an **intro** (introduction) and sometimes an **outro** (like a coda). Many songs will include a **bridge** (a contrasting section) for variety.

12-bar blues:

Phrase 1	I	I	I	I
Phrase 2	IV	IV	I	I
Phrase 3	V	IV	I	I

The 12-bar blues is the 12-bar chord progression given above. It is used in many **blues** and **jazz** pieces.

1. What are the **three** main sections in sonata form?
2. What is different about the repeat of Section A in a da capo aria?
3. 32-bar song form is made up of four phrases. Which one of these phrases is different to the others?
4. What is the name for the following structure: ABACADA?

TIMBRE

'Timbre' refers to the tone colour or sound quality of the music – what instruments are playing it and how it sounds. Questions on timbre may ask you to name the melody instrument or describe particular instrumental techniques.

INSTRUMENTS

Try to make sure you can recognise the sounds of the different instruments below. (World music instruments aren't included here – see the 'World music' section on page 50 for information on these.)

Strings	■ Violin ■ Double bass	■ Viola ■ Harp	■ Cello ■ Guitar
Woodwind	■ Flute ■ Saxophone	■ Clarinet ■ Oboe	■ Piccolo ■ Bassoon
Brass	■ Trumpet ■ Horn	■ Trombone ■ Tuba	
Percussion	■ Xylophone ■ Glockenspiel ■ Snare drum	■ Timpani ■ Bass drum	
Keyboard instruments	■ Piano	■ Organ	■ Harpsichord
Voice	■ Soprano ■ Alto ■ Baritone	■ Treble ■ Countertenor ■ Bass	■ Mezzo soprano ■ Tenor

INSTRUMENTAL TECHNIQUES

You should be able to explain, and identify by ear, some of the more common instrumental techniques listed below:

Strings:

- **Arco**: **bow** the strings
- **Pizzicato**: **pluck** the strings
- **Con sordino**: play with a **mute** (a direction also used for **brass** players)
- **Tremolo**: rapidly and continuously repeat a note
- **Double stopping**: play two or more notes at once (to create a **chord**).

Wind and brass:

- **Slurred**: notes are played **smoothly**
- **Tongued**: notes are played **separately**.

Drums:

- **Fills**: a short passage of music that **fills in a gap** between different phrases of a melody.

Voice:

- **Falsetto**: a technique used by men to sing in a **high range**
- **Vibrato**: a technique that makes the pitch of a note **waver** for expressive effect.

TECHNOLOGY AND TIMBRE

Popular music, and club dance music in particular, often makes use of **electronic instruments**. Four of the ones most commonly used are:

- **Drum machine**: an electronic instrument that **replicates** the sounds of different **percussion instruments**.
- **Mixing desk**: an electronic device used to **combine** (or 'mix') **different audio signals**, which can then be **manipulated**.
- **Sampler**: an electronic instrument that allows you to **alter and manipulate samples**. A **sample** is a short portion taken from an existing recording, which is then included in a new track. Almost anything can be sampled: a drum rhythm, a guitar riff, a vocal line or even speech from a TV show.
- **Synthesiser**: an electronic instrument that can be controlled through a **keyboard**, which allows you to manipulate the sounds produced and add digital effects. Most electronic music includes **synthesised** sounds.

You might also come across the following digital effects and techniques:

- **Reverb**: makes the music sound as if it was **recorded in a resonant space**.
- **Delay**: creates the effect of an **echo**.
- **Distortion**: alters the sound of an instrument so it becomes **rougher** and **harsher**.
- **Chorus**: **thickens** the sound by superimposing similar versions of the same track (e.g. chorus on a solo voice sounds like several people singing the same line).
- **Panning**: alters the **placement of a sound** from left to right of the listener.
- **Quantising**: a process that **fixes notes** into a **rhythmic grid**, increasing **rhythmic accuracy** but sometimes losing some expression.

TEST YOURSELF

1. What does 'con sordino' mean, and which instruments can it apply to?
2. What is a sample?
3. What term is used for the digital effect that can make a solo voice sound like several people singing?
4. What performance direction tells a violinist to pluck their strings?

IMPORTANT REMINDER

The rest of this guide focuses on all of the topics from which music might be taken in the exam. A little background and contextual information is provided for each topic, to help you gain an overview of it and to help you answer questions in which you have to identify the genre or culture that the musical extract is taken from. However, remember that the exam focuses on your **listening skills** and most of the questions will primarily test you on your knowledge of the **elements of music**. With this in mind, focus on listening to the pieces discussed under each topic and picking out their main musical features.

The Western classical tradition

Baroque orchestral music

The Baroque period of music lasted from around **1600** to **1750**. The word 'Baroque' was used to describe things that were ornate and extravagant, and Baroque music is often very **decorative**, with ornamented melody lines and complex counterpoint.

The Baroque **orchestra** developed at the end of the 17th century. Compared to orchestras in later years, the Baroque orchestra was fairly **small**. The orchestra would usually be directed by the **harpsichord player** or **principal violinist** instead of a conductor.

Dates: 1700–1750 (the late Baroque period)

Main centre: Western Europe

Main composers: Vivaldi, Handel, Bach

Main genres: concerto grosso, concerto, orchestral suite

Examples: *The Four Seasons* by Vivaldi, Concerto Grosso in D minor, Op. 3 No. 5 by Handel, Orchestral Suite No. 3 in D major by Bach

A Baroque orchestra usually consists of:

- **String** instruments (violins, violas, cellos, double bass)
- **Continuo** instruments – a small group of musicians who play the **continuo part**, which is a bass line with an indication of how to improvise harmonies. There is usually a **keyboard** instrument (harpsichord or organ), with one or more **bass** instruments (such as cello or double bass).

Some of the following instruments might also have been added:

- **Woodwind** (flutes or recorders, oboes, bassoons)
- **Brass** (trumpets, horns)
- **Timpani**.

KEY FEATURES OF BAROQUE MUSIC

1. **Simple, diatonic** harmonies
2. Movements that keep the **same mood** throughout
3. **Terraced dynamics** – changes in volume are sudden rather than gradual
4. **Ornamentation** – melodies are often highly decorated
5. Complex **contrapuntal** writing in some places
6. The presence of a **harpsichord** in almost all orchestral music of the period.

♫ Listen to...

CONCERTO GROSSO IN D MINOR, OP. 3 NO. 11 (FIRST MOVEMENT, 'ALLEGRO') BY VIVALDI

In a concerto grosso, the orchestra divides into two groups: the **concertino** (a small group of soloists) and the **ripieno** (the rest of the orchestra).

In this work, the concertino is made up of two violins, cello and harpsichord. The ripieno consists of violins, viola, double bass and continuo.

Listen out for:

- ■ The alternation between passages for **ripieno** (e.g. 0:00–0:56) and **concertino** (e.g. 0:56–1:18)
- ■ The **terraced dynamics** (e.g. f at 2:30–2:32 followed by p at 2:32–2:35)
- ■ The **contrapuntal textures** (can you spot where the first four imitative entries come in, and in what order?)
- ■ The **dominant pedal note** in the cello and double bass (2:30–3:01).

ORCHESTRAL SUITE NO. 3 IN D MAJOR (GIGUE) BY BACH

A **suite** is a collection of short pieces. Most suites are made up of dances – the last movement of this suite is a **gigue**, which is a lively dance in compound time.

Listen out for:

- ■ The **instrumentation** (strings, harpsichord, bassoon, oboes, trumpets, timpani)
- ■ The **compound metre** ($\frac{6}{8}$) and **fast tempo**
- ■ The use of **melodic sequence** (e.g. in the violins and trumpets there is a descending sequence at 0:10–0:15)
- ■ The **terraced dynamics** created when the trumpets and timpani drop out or come back in (compare 0:00–0:05 with 0:05–0:10)
- ■ The **binary form** (**A** at 0:00, repeated at 0:28, is followed by **B** at 0:56, repeated at 1:50)
- ■ The **modulation** from the tonic (D major) to the dominant (A major) in the A section. Section B starts in the dominant and modulates back to the tonic at the end.

1. What is the name given to the group of instruments that play the bass line and harmonic filling in Baroque music?
2. Which **two** of the following instruments might be found in a Baroque orchestra?
    (a) guitar   (b) harpsichord   (c) recorder   (d) saxophone   (e) tuba
3. Baroque orchestral music is sometimes contrapuntal. What does this mean?

The concerto

A concerto is a work for **solo instrument** accompanied by **orchestra**. It is usually in **three** movements (fast–slow–fast).

In the Baroque period, the **concerto grosso** was a popular form, which alternated passages for a few soloists with passages for the whole orchestra. The **solo concerto** replaced this in popularity during the Classical period. Concertos have since been written throughout the Romantic period and 20th century, for a wide range of solo instruments.

Dates: late 17th century–present day

Main centres: Western Europe and America

Main composers: most composers from the Baroque period onwards (e.g. Vivaldi, Bach, Mozart, Brahms, Stravinsky)

Main types of piece: piano concerto (Classical period onwards), violin concerto (all periods), concerto grosso (Baroque period)

Examples: Oboe Concerto in A minor by Vivaldi, Piano Concerto No. 5 by Beethoven, Violin Concerto No. 1 by Bruch

KEY FEATURES

- Alternations between **solo sections** (in which the soloist plays alone or with a light accompaniment) and **tutti sections** (for the full orchestra)
- A **cadenza** – an unaccompanied passage for the soloist, which usually comes at the end of the first movement in concertos from the Classical period onwards
- **Virtuosic** playing, with rapid scales and arpeggios, extreme registers, large leaps and ornamentation (especially in the cadenza)
- Themes being **exchanged** between the soloist and orchestra.

🎧 Listen to...

TRUMPET CONCERTO IN E♭ MAJOR (THIRD MOVEMENT) BY HAYDN

This concerto was written in 1796, and is one of Haydn's most famous works.

Listen out for:

- ■ The **orchestral introduction**: this sets the tempo, key and mood of the movement, and introduces the main theme
- ■ The trumpet's **first entry** (0:38) – the orchestral accompaniment is much **quieter and lighter**, using fewer instruments
- ■ The orchestra **taking over** the trumpet's material and playing at a louder dynamic in between the trumpet's phrases
- ■ The **rondo** form – how many times does the main theme return?
- ■ The trumpet and violins taking it in turns to play the melodic material at 1:22–1:35, creating a **musical dialogue**.

TEST YOURSELF

1. How many movements does a concerto normally contain?
2. What is the term for a virtuosic, unaccompanied passage played by the soloist?
3. What is the difference between a concerto grosso and a solo concerto?

Music for voices

Some form of vocal music exists in every culture around the world, and it often has a history that spans centuries. Even within the Western classical tradition there is an incredibly diverse range of vocal music on offer, but we can perhaps group this into three main categories:

1. Works for choir

Choral works include the mass, oratorio, cantata and anthem. These pieces are often set to **religious texts** and performed in a **church or cathedral** (although many concerts of choral music are also given in other venues).

A choir is usually made up of **sopranos**, **altos**, **tenors** and **basses**. They may be unaccompanied (**a cappella**) or accompanied by an orchestra, organ, piano or other ensemble.

Large-scale choral works often include a number of **choruses** (for the whole choir) and **arias** (for soloists).

2. Solo songs

Classical solo songs are often accompanied by **piano**. They are usually performed in a **small concert hall** or **recital room**.

The **Lied** (plural Leider) is a popular type of solo song from the Romantic period, set to German poetry. Lieder are usually quite short, but can sometimes be joined together to form a longer **song cycle**.

3. Opera

An opera is a **staged drama** in which all of the action is expressed through music. In this sense an opera is similar to a musical, except that operas are based on a classical rather than popular style. An opera is usually performed by **vocal soloists** and a **chorus**, who are accompanied by an **orchestra**.

KEY FEATURES TO LISTEN OUT FOR

1. Type of voice

Female	Soprano	High
	Mezzo soprano	Medium
	Alto	Low
Male	(Treble	A boy's high voice – equivalent to a soprano)
	(Countertenor	A male alto)
	Tenor	High
	Baritone	Medium
	Bass	Low

2. Vocal techniques

These include falsetto and vibrato (vibrato is nearly always used by solo singers, particularly in opera, but is less common in a choir).

3. Structure

Three forms specific to songs are strophic, through-composed and the da capo aria, although songs can also use different types of structure, such as binary or ternary form.

4. Text setting and word painting

A musical technique that attempts to illustrate a word or phrase in the text is called **word painting**. A few examples are:

- A rising phrase for the word 'ascending'
- Held notes for words that describe stillness and calm
- Major chords to suggest triumph and happiness
- Jumping, chromatic lines for words that depict suffering and pain.

Try to identify whether the word setting is **syllabic** (each syllable is sung to a different note) or **melismatic** (one syllable is sung to several notes, creating a **melisma**).

In opera of the 19th century and later, composers often used **leitmotivs** – musical ideas that are used to represent a person or object, which return throughout the piece in slightly different forms.

 **Listen to…**

'I HAVE TO GO FROM PUB TO PUB' FROM PETER GRIMES BY BRITTEN

This is a short scene from a 20th-century **opera** set in a 19th-century fishing village. A **carter** is being asked to fetch a new apprentice for Peter Grimes, a fisherman who is suspected by the villagers of having killed his previous apprentice. The carter does not want to fetch the apprentice, but **Ellen Orford**, a friend of Peter Grimes, offers to accompany the carter. **Balstrode** supports her in this but the **villagers** are angry.

Listen out for:

- The **syllabic** word-setting: this enables the words to be heard clearly
- The different vocal forces:
  - The carter, sung by a **bass** (0:00–0:21)
  - The villagers, sung by a **chorus** (0:22–0:26)
  - Ellen Orford, sung by a **soprano** (0:35–0:43)
  - Balstrode, sung by a **baritone** (1:34–1:37).
- The **dramatic** nature of the music, which helps to **reinforce** what the characters are saying:
  - The carter's music has a **lurching, dotted rhythm** and a rustic feel, accompanied by **tambourine, pizzicato strings** and **bassoon**: this sounds like an old horse and cart trundling along a rough road (0:00–0:21)
  - When Ellen Orford first sings, her music is much **gentler**, with **high strings, flute** and **harp** (0:35–1:05)
  - She then **copies** the carter's music, singing a **rising sequence**, as she tries to persuade him to let her accompany him (1:05–1:34)
  - When Balstrode enters, his music is **rhythmic** and more **forceful**, accompanied by **timpani** (1:34–1:37), suggesting a strong character
  - The chorus then has a **rhythmic, syncopated** idea in **homophony**, whose dramatic **crescendo** reflects their growing anger (1:37–1:56)
  - Ellen Orford's entry at 1:57 is **loud** and in a **high register**: this illustrates her impatience and anger with the villagers.

Chamber music

'Chamber music' is a term used for **instrumental music** performed by a **small group of players** (usually between two and eight). It is so-called because it was originally performed in a 'chamber' or small room, rather than a larger building such as a cathedral or concert hall. Although chamber music has been written from before the Baroque period to the present day, it was particularly popular in the **Classical period**.

Dates: 1600–present day

Main centres: Western Europe and America

Main composers: most composers from the Baroque period to the present day, e.g. Handel, Beethoven, Schumann

Place of performance: a small concert hall or private room

Examples: Piano Quintet in A major ('The Trout') by Schubert, String Quartet in G minor, Op. 10 by Debussy

MAIN TYPES OF ENSEMBLE

In the **Baroque period**, chamber music was written for many different combinations of instruments, although an ensemble would usually have a **continuo** part (for harpsichord and cello).

Standard groupings started to form in the **Classical period**, and each ensemble would be described by how many instruments it contained (i.e. a 'trio' for three, a 'quartet' for four and so on). The most popular groupings are given below (the most important one of these to remember is the **string quartet**):

String trio	violin, viola, cello
String quartet	2 violins, viola, cello
String quintet	2 violins, 2 violas, cello / 2 violins, viola, 2 cellos
Piano trio	violin, cello, piano
Piano quartet	violin, viola, cello, piano
Piano quintet	2 violins, viola, cello, piano / violin, viola, cello, double bass, piano
Wind quintet	flute, oboe, clarinet, bassoon, horn

MAIN STRUCTURES AND FORMS

- **Baroque** chamber music often consisted of a mixture of slow and fast movements, some of which were based on **binary-form dances**.
- During the **Classical period**, much chamber music followed a **four-movement** plan.
- From the **Romantic period** onwards, structures became more varied and freer.

KEY FEATURES TO LISTEN OUT FOR

1. **Instrumentation** – can you work out what type of chamber group is playing?
2. Each instrument's **role** within the ensemble in any given passage: are they accompanying, providing a bass line, playing a melody, doubling another part, or filling out the inner parts in a texture?
3. Material being **passed between** instruments, creating a musical dialogue (perhaps through imitation).
4. Special **instrumental techniques**, such as the use of pizzicato or double stopping.
5. The **general musical style** (Baroque, Classical, Romantic or 20th century), and the features of the harmony, melody, rhythm, tempo, and so on associated with those styles.

♫ Listen to...

PIANO TRIO IN D MINOR, OP. 49 NO. 1 (FIRST MOVEMENT) BY MENDELSSOHN

This work was written in 1839 and is one of Mendelssohn's most popular chamber works.

Listen out for:

- The **instrumentation** (violin, cello, piano)
- The **texture** (mainly **melody and accompaniment**, although we can find other examples such as **homophony** at 0:23–0:35, and **imitation** between the violin and cello at 0:46–0:58)
- The **sonata-form** structure:
    - The **first subject** in the **exposition** is the opening theme played by the cello
    - The **second subject** is another lyrical theme introduced by the cello at 1:50, but this time in **A major** (the dominant)
    - The **development** explores both themes further
    - The **recapitulation** at 5:52 combines the opening cello theme with a violin countermelody.
- The **different roles** the instruments take at different times, for example:
    - Cello melody, piano accompaniment (0:00–0:15)
    - Piano melody and accompaniment, with a cello pedal note (0:35–0:39)
    - Piano melody and accompaniment, with violin and cello countermelodies (1:30–1:38).
- The **virtuoso** writing, for example:
    - Fast **scales** and **broken chords** in the piano (0:59–1:22)
    - Rapid **repeated triplets** in the violin and cello (3:11–3:17).

TEST YOURSELF

1. Which instruments make up a string quartet?
2. The piano is a common instrument in chamber music ensembles. Name a chamber music ensemble of three or more players that includes a piano.
3. The last movement of a Classical chamber work is often in rondo form. What is rondo form?

The sonata

In the Baroque period, the term 'sonata' was used for works that were played rather than sung, but with no set form or number of movements. In the **Classical period**, the sonata became a **multi-movement work** for a **solo instrument**.

> **Dates**: 1600–present day
>
> **Main centres**: Western Europe and America
>
> **Main composers**: most composers from the Baroque period onwards, e.g. Scarlatti, Mozart, Beethoven, Schumann, Brahms
>
> **Main types of ensemble**: solo piano, or solo instrument and piano (e.g. violin and piano, or clarinet and piano)
>
> **Place of performance**: a small concert hall or recital room
>
> **Examples**: Piano Sonata in C♯ minor ('Moonlight') by Beethoven, Violin Sonata in A major, K. 526 by Mozart

STRUCTURE AND FORM

Sonatas in the Classical and Romantic periods usually had **three** or **four** movements, often following this plan:

1.	Sonata form	Fast
2.	Variation form or ternary form	Slow
3.	Minuet and trio, or scherzo and trio	Fast, in $\frac{3}{4}$
4.	Rondo form or sonata form	Fast

(A sonata in three movements will omit one of the middle two movements.)

The first movement, in **sonata form**, will itself have the following structure:

Exposition		Development	Recapitulation	
1st subject (tonic)	2nd subject (dominant/ relative major)	(various keys)	1st subject (tonic)	2nd subject (tonic)

There are three main sections here:

1. **Exposition**: two main themes (called the **first subject** and **second subject**) are presented. They are in **different keys** (usually tonic and dominant, or tonic and relative major if the piece is in a minor key). They also tend to have **contrasting moods** (e.g. lively and loud vs. sustained and quiet). The entire exposition is usually repeated before the development is played.

2. **Development**: ideas from the exposition are **developed freely**, passing through several keys.
3. **Recapitulation**: the **first subject** and **second subject** are played again, this time both in the tonic key. The whole piece is usually rounded off with a short **coda**.

🎧 Listen to...

PIANO SONATA IN C MAJOR, K. 309 BY MOZART

This work was written in 1777, and is one of Mozart's earlier sonatas for piano.

Listen out for:

First movement:

◼ The **sonata form**:

Exposition	0:00	**First subject** in the tonic key (C major)
	1:00	**Second subject** in the dominant key (G major)
	1:39	**Repeat** of exposition
Development	3:12	The music passes through **several keys** (e.g. D minor and A minor), developing the first subject in particular
Recapitulation	4:11	**First subject** in the tonic key (C major)
	5:08	**Second subject** in the tonic key (C major)

◼ The **fast tempo** (allegro) and $\frac{4}{4}$ metre
◼ **Contrasts of dynamics** between $\boldsymbol{f}$ (e.g. 0:06) and $\boldsymbol{p}$ (e.g. 0:09)
◼ Use of **ornamentation** such as **appoggiaturas** (e.g. in the first phrase at 0:11–0:12), and **trills** (1:28–1:29).

Second movement:

◼ The **slow tempo** (andante) – this provides contrast to the first movement
◼ The **new key** (F major, the subdominant), which again provides contrast
◼ The **first melody** (0:00–1:03), which is heard **four times** in total; listen to how it is **varied** each time with different **ornamentation**:
  ◼ 1:04–2:03: the melody is decorated with **acciaccaturas**, **triplets** and other short notes
  ◼ 2:50–3:20: the melody is decorated with **chromatic notes**, and **dotted rhythms** in which the short notes precede the long notes
  ◼ 4:06–end: the melody is decorated with **scalic passages** and extra notes.

Third movement:

- The **fast tempo** (allegretto), which contrasts with the second movement and balances the first movement
- A return to the **tonic key** of C major
- The **rondo structure** – the rondo theme, first heard at 0:00, also returns at 2:14, 4:34 and in a shortened version at 5:57
- The **broken-chord accompaniment** in the left hand
- The opening theme, based on **descending scales** (0:00–0:28) is balanced by a melody that uses **rising arpeggios** (0:29–0:46).

TEST YOURSELF

1. Place these sections of a sonata-form movement in the correct order:
   (a) development   (b) exposition   (c) recapitulation
2. What happens in the development section of a sonata-form movement?
3. When a sonata has **four** movements, what form is the third movement usually in?

Popular music of the 20th and 21st centuries

Blues

The blues is a style of music that was developed by the **rural African-American population** in the **southern states of America** during the **late 19th and early 20th centuries**. The first blues musicians were descendants of the slaves that worked on the cotton and sugar plantations, who had been imported from **West Africa**. As a result, blues music shares a number of characteristics with African music, such as flattened blue notes and call-and-response phrases.

Early blues music was usually performed by a **solo singer accompanied by guitar**, and the songs were often about deprivation and hardship. As the popularity of the blues spread, musicians moved away from the rural south to the cities and the music eventually became **more dance-orientated**, with the addition of **jazz instruments** and a **drum kit**. As the genre developed it influenced many other styles of popular music, including rock and roll, R 'n' B and soul.

KEY FEATURES

Rhythm and metre	▪ Usually in $\frac{4}{4}$ ▪ **Syncopation** and **rhythmic flexibility** are common in the melody ▪ The accompaniment often uses **swung rhythms** and **triplets**.
Harmony and tonality	▪ The **12-bar blues pattern** is based on the following chord pattern: I I I I, IV IV I I, V IV I I ▪ These basic triads are often extended into **7th chords**.
Texture and melody	▪ The melody can often sound quite **improvisatory** in style ▪ It is frequently based around a **limited range** of notes and is fairly **repetitive** ▪ **Four-bar phrases** are common ▪ **Call and response** may sometimes be used ▪ Melodies are based on the **blues scale**, a **hexatonic** scale that includes **blue notes** – the flattened third, fifth and seventh degrees of the scale: ▪ The texture is usually **melody and accompaniment**.

Timbre	■ A **rough**, **growling** style of singing is common ■ This is sometimes **imitated** by the **brass section** ■ **Popular instruments** include: voice, guitar, piano, double bass, drum kit, saxophone, trumpet, trombone and harmonica.
Structure and form	■ The **12-bar blues pattern** is **repeated** throughout the song ■ **Each statement** of the 12-bar sequence forms a **verse** ■ A song may contain three or more verses, with an **instrumental solo** replacing a verse for variety ■ It is common for the lyrics of each verse to consist of **three phrases** (each lasting four bars) in **AAB** form.

🎧 Listen to...

'I BELIEVE I'LL DUST MY BROOM' BY ROBERT JOHNSTON

Robert Johnston is a famous early blues musician – this song was recorded in 1936.

Characteristic features include:

■ A variation on the **12-bar blues pattern** (listen to the lowest notes in the guitar):

I	I	I	I	IV	IV	I	I	V	IV	I	V
E	E	E	E	A	A	E	E	B	A	E	B

■ The combination of **acoustic guitar** and **voice**
■ The **blue notes** and **flexible rhythms** in the melody, which has an **improvised feel**
■ The **triplets** and **swung rhythms** in the accompaniment
■ The **guitar riff** that links together different verses, based on a characteristic descending chromatic scale
■ The use of **7th chords** in the harmony
■ The **AAB** structure of the lyrics.

'GOIN' HOME' BY FATS DOMINO

Fats Domino is a popular blues musician who still lives in New Orleans today – 'Goin' Home' was recorded in the 1950s, one of his most successful decades.

Listen out for:

- The standard **12-bar blues pattern**
- The **line-up** of voice, electric guitar, piano, saxophones, drum kit and double bass
- The **AAB** lyric structure
- The **limited range** of the vocal line, which is based around only three notes
- The **repeated triplets** in the accompaniment
- The **raucous** saxophone solo.

TEST YOURSELF

1. How are the lyrics of a 12-bar blues often structured?
2. Describe the standard chord progression used in a 12-bar blues.
3. What is a blue note?
4. Which **two** rhythms are often used in the accompaniment to a blues song?

Popular music of the 1960s

The late **1950s** were dominated by **rock and roll**. Although its popularity declined in the 1960s, it had a huge influence on **British bands** such as **The Beatles**, **The Who** and **The Rolling Stones**. In America, **soul** was the most popular form of black music, heavily promoted by the **Motown record label**. Towards the end of the 1960s, more **experimental styles** such as **psychedelic rock** were created, influenced by the latest technological developments.

KEY FEATURES

Rhythm and metre	<ul><li>Usually in $\frac{4}{4}$ with a **strong sense of pulse**</li><li>The **backbeats** (beats 2 and 4) are often **accented**</li><li>**Syncopation** is common.</li></ul>
Harmony and tonality	<ul><li>Most songs are based on **simple diatonic harmonies**, with **occasional 7th chords**</li><li>**Progressive bands** used **more adventurous harmonies**, **dissonances** and **modulations** to unlikely keys.</li></ul>

Texture and melody	■ The texture is usually **melody and accompaniment** with a **rhythmic backing**: 　　■ The **drum kit** provides the **beat** 　　■ The **bass guitar** plays the **bass line** 　　■ The **rhythm guitar** strums **chords** 　　■ The **lead guitar** plays **countermelodies** and **solos** 　　■ The **voice** sings the **main melody**. ■ Melodies are usually **catchy** and **repetitive**, in **four-bar phrases**.
Timbre and dynamics	■ **Common instruments** include voice, backing singers, guitar, bass guitar, drum kit, horn section and the Hammond organ ■ More **experimental bands** often used **less common instruments**, such as sitar or timpani ■ **Production effects** such as **chorus**, **reverb** and **distortion** became more common towards the end of the decade ■ **Compression** is added to many recordings to **even out the dynamics**.
Structure and form	■ **Verse-chorus structure** is the most common form. It is usually made up of: 　　■ An **intro** (usually just instrumental) 　　■ Different **verses** 　　■ A repeated **chorus** 　　■ A **bridge** (a contrasting section) 　　■ An **outro** (like a coda).

◠ Listen to...

'DANCING IN THE STREET' BY MARTHA AND THE VANDELLAS

The **Motown record label** produced a huge number of hits in the 1960s, using tried and trusted formulae to guarantee profits. This song, a classic **soul hit** from 1964, is a good example of the 1960s' Motown sound.

Listen out for:

■ The $\frac{4}{4}$ metre and **heavy accents** on the **backbeats** (beats 2 and 4)
■ The **large instrumental forces** and the **warm, reverberant sound** they create
■ The use of a **horn section**, which is typical of Motown records
■ The **catchy vocal solo** and **soul style of singing** which features **ornamentation** and **melismas**
■ The **short melodic solos** in the **trumpets** and **other instruments** between phrases of the vocal solo.

'MY GENERATION' BY THE WHO

The British rock band The Who was originally a **blues band** and this song shows many influences of the blues. 'My Generation', released in 1965, became an unofficial anthem of the mods, a British teenage movement united by their tastes in fashion and music.

Listen out for:

- The use of **bass guitar, electric guitar, drums** and **male singer** – a line-up typical of 1960s British bands
- The **blues-influenced singing and harmonies,** with the use of **blue notes** in the vocal line
- The **backbeats** accented by **snare and hand claps**
- The **call and response** between **solo vocalist and backing singers**
- The **bass solo** at 0:56 and the **virtuoso drum solo** at 2:26.

TEST YOURSELF

1. Describe **one** feature of the singing and **one** feature of the instrumentation that is typical of soul music produced by the Motown record label.
2. Popular music of the 1960s often features strong backbeats. What are backbeats?
3. Name the typical line-up that would be found in a British band such as The Beatles.
4. Describe the basic structure of a song in verse-chorus form.

Rock music

Rock music developed in the **1960s** out of **rock and roll** and **rhythm and blues**. Groups such as **The Who** started to use more and more **powerful amplifiers** and a **distorted guitar tone**, coupled with a macho style of singing and over-the-top stage performances. Their sound was copied by 1970s groups such as **Led Zeppelin** and **Queen**, and by the middle of the decade, live performances were filling enormous venues such as football stadia.

There are many different types of rock music, including heavy metal, progressive rock, punk rock and grunge. You won't be expected to know the characteristics of each of these styles in detail; concentrate instead on the key features of what all rock styles have in common: a **guitar-dominated sound**, which frequently uses **distortion**, a **heavy drum beat**, powerful **amplification** and a **male-dominated, macho** style of singing.

Characteristic features include:

Rhythm and metre	■ Usually in $\frac{4}{4}$ ■ Often with a **heavy emphasis** on the backbeats or all four beats.
Harmony and tonality	■ Frequently based around chords **I**, **IV** and **V** ■ **Power chords** are common (a chord that includes the root and fifth, but omits the third, e.g. a chord of G major with just the notes G and D) ■ Heavy metal uses some **dissonant** intervals such as tritones.

Texture and melody	■ Often a **melody and accompaniment** texture with:
	   ■ **Drums** providing a strong pulse
	   ■ **Bass guitar** adding a bass line
	   ■ **Rhythm guitar** playing chords
	   ■ **Solo guitar** providing countermelodies and solos
	   ■ **Vocalist** singing the main melody.
	■ The vocal melody is usually **repetitive** and **catchy**. Any guitar solos often feature **virtuoso** playing, with fast runs, pitch bends and special guitar techniques.

Timbre and dynamics	■ Much rock music is dominated by a powerful **electric guitar** sound, which is often **distorted** ■ Singers are almost always **male** and sing in a '**macho**', rough style ■ In live concerts rock music is generally played at a **very loud dynamic**.
Structure and form	■ A **verse-chorus** structure is common, with a **guitar solo** in the bridge.

⌒ Listen to...

'WHATEVER YOU WANT' BY STATUS QUO

Status Quo is an English rock band that was particularly popular during the 1970s. 'Whatever You Want' was released in 1979, and reached the UK top ten.

Listen out for:

■ The **guitar solo** that opens the song, which has a rough, aggressive sound due to the use of **distortion**
■ The **driving rhythm** on the rhythm guitar at 0:26, based on a **power chord** of D (the notes D and A)
■ The entry of the **drums** at 0:57, with an emphasis on **all four beats** (bass drum) but particularly the **backbeats** (snare drum)

- The **repetitive melody**, with a **very narrow range**
- The **simple chord progressions** – the main melody, which lasts for eight bars, is accompanied just by chords of **D** and **A major** (tonic and dominant)
- The **guitar solo** in the middle of the song, which is more **virtuosic** than the vocal melody, with **varied rhythms** and a **wider range**.

TEST YOURSELF

1. Which instrument dominates rock music?
2. Name **two** musical features of rock music that lend it a 'macho' quality.
3. Name the main effect that is usually applied to the guitar part in rock music.

R 'n' B

R 'n' B is a contemporary form of **African-American popular music** that mixes elements of **hip hop** and **funk** with a **soul-influenced** style of singing. It relies, like hip hop, on **technology** for most of its instrumental sounds. But although it may sometimes contain **rap**, R 'n' B is generally a much **smoother, laid-back** style than hip hop.

Characteristic features include:

Rhythm and metre	Usually in $\frac{4}{4}$ with a **laid-back tempo** A **tight, syncopated rhythmic backing** is programmed using a **drum machine** or **sequencer**.
Harmony and tonality	Mostly **simple, diatonic harmonies**.
Texture and melody	The **melody and accompaniment** texture is frequently made up of: a rhythmic backing track; a synthesised bass line; another instrument to fill in the harmony; a vocal melody The vocal lines often use **ornamentation** and **melismas** Melodies are usually **simple** and **catchy**.
Timbre and dynamics	The **instrumental backing** is usually made up from **synthesised and sampled sounds** Singers are often **female** and have a **smooth style of singing** influenced by **soul** **Rapping** will sometimes appear.
Structure and form	Songs usually have a **verse-chorus** structure.

🎧 Listen to...

'ANGELS CRY' BY MARIAH CAREY

This song was released as a single in 2010 and was co-written by one of the most influential R 'n' B artists, Mariah Carey.

Characteristic features include:

- The **soulful style of singing**
- The extensive use of **vocal overdubbing**
- The use of a **simple, repeated chord progression**
- The **programmed drum track** with **synthesised hand claps** on **beats 2 and 4**
- The use of 'soft' sounding instruments such as **piano** and **chimes**.

'TRY AGAIN' BY AALIYAH

'Try Again' was released in 2000. It originally appeared in the martial arts film *Romeo Must Die*, which Aaliyah also acted in.

Listen out for:

- The **tight, syncopated drum track** (programmed with a **drum machine**)
- The prominence of **overdubbed vocal lines** which create variety through the use of different textures
- The use of **samples**, such as the **spoken vocal sample** at the start
- The **improvised vocal phrases** towards the end that include **melismas**.

TEST YOURSELF

1. Which type of popular music heavily influenced the **vocal** style of R 'n' B, and what effect has this had on the vocal lines?
2. Name **two** ways in which music technology is often used in R 'n' B.

Hip hop

Hip hop is a style of **black popular music** that has its origins in the **street culture** of **1970s New York**. Its main feature is **rapping**: speaking rhythmically (often with rhyme) to a beat.

Hip hop was different from, say, rock music as it relied on **technology** rather than live instrumentalists. Early forms of hip hop consisted of rapping over a backing provided by **DJs mixing and scratching records**. This backing part was replaced by the use of **drum machines**, **samplers** and **sequencers** as technology developed.

Characteristic features include:

Rhythm and metre	▪ Usually in $\frac{4}{4}$ ▪ The words of a **rap** are often **quick** and **syncopated**, creating **cross rhythms** with the backing track (and contrasting with a **sung chorus** that usually has **simpler rhythms**) ▪ Hip hop frequently uses **breakbeat** rhythms: samples of syncopated drum solos from funk or jazz music ▪ **Complex** but **repetitive** rhythmic patterns are produced by layers of **sampled and looped sounds**.
Harmony and tonality	▪ As the music is often based on just a rhythmic rap over a drum loop, there may be **little use of harmony** in some songs, the emphasis being on the rhythm ▪ When harmony appears, it will probably be a **simple, looped chord pattern**.
Texture and melody	▪ **Layered** textures are built up from **loops** ▪ The **chorus** of a hip-hop song is often based on a very **simple, repetitive melody**.
Timbre and dynamics	▪ The instrumental backing is made up of **synthesised and sampled sounds** ▪ Over a rap there may be **other vocal sounds** such as shouts or singing from a backing group.
Structure and form	▪ Songs usually have a **verse-chorus** structure, or a structure built up from **layers of loops** similar to dance music.

◯ Listen to...

'I KNOW YOU GOT SOUL' BY ERIC B. AND RAKIM

This track, released in 1987, samples the original 1971 version of a song by Bobby Byrd.

Listen out for:

- The **syncopated rhythms** of the rap
- The **breaks** where the backing drops out, leaving the vocalist on their own
- The repeated **three-note melodic riff** that **lasts for most of the song**
- The **drum track** made up of a **looped, breakbeat rhythm**
- The use of **scratching**, a DJ technique that produces a squeaky sound.

'MS. JACKSON' (RADIO MIX) BY OUTKAST

'Ms. Jackson', released in 2000, samples a song from 1977 called 'Strawberry Letter 23'.

Characteristic features include:

- The mixture of a **sung chorus** and **rapped verses**
- The **quick, syncopated rhythms** of the rap
- The **catchy melody** of the chorus
- The use of a **sampled drum loop** and a **simple, repeated chord pattern** that lasts for most of the song
- The use of a **sustained, synthesised bass line** made up of only **three notes** which **repeats** throughout most of the song
- The important role played by **music technology** on the track, particularly the frequent **overdubbing** and **use of samples**.

TEST YOURSELF

1. The main feature of hip hop is rapping. What is rapping?
2. Describe **two** differences between the instrumentation of a typical hip hop track and a typical rock track.
3. Describe **two** musical similarities and **two** musical differences between R 'n' B and hip hop.

Music theatre

The **modern musical**, which developed in the **1920s**, grew out of **operetta** (light opera) and **variety shows** (an evening's entertainment mixing comedy, dancing, songs and magic). Early musicals were collections of popular songs linked together by acted scenes to make a story. Over time, the acted and sung elements became more successfully integrated and the stories more weighty, with musicals such as *Porgy and Bess* and *West Side Story* addressing themes such as racial segregation and gang violence. The music became more sophisticated, too, with composers drawing on the rhythms and harmonies of 20th-century classical music and jazz.

KEY FEATURES

- Musicals usually consist of **alternating sections** of **spoken dialogue** and **songs**.
- They tend to contain a variety of **different types of song**, such as ballads (slow and emotional), patter songs (fast and comic) and production numbers (involving most of the cast).
- Songs are often sung in a **theatrical way**. The **accents** of the characters are **preserved** and recorded performances often sound like they are being **acted out**. Musicals are often performed by **actors** rather than classically trained singers.
- Songs can be for **different combinations of singers**, from solo songs and duets and trios, up to whole cast numbers.
- The music **depicts** or **complements** the **on-stage drama**, often expressing the **mood and feelings of the character** singing the song.
- The **accompaniment** is usually played by a band or small orchestra.
- The music is nearly always in a **popular style**, sometimes influenced by **jazz** or **rock**.
- The **harmony** is usually **diatonic**, but **richer** than in **pop music**; **contrasts of key** and **modulation** are common.
- Melodies are designed to be **memorable** and **catchy** and so contain **lots of repetition**.
- Singers often use **rubato** to make the words as **expressive** as possible.
- **32-bar song form** is very common in musicals, in which a short verse is followed by a 32-bar chorus made up of four eight-bar phrases in the order AABA.

🎧 Listen to...

'I COULD HAVE DANCED ALL NIGHT' BY FREDERICK LOEWE

This song is from the musical *My Fair Lady*, which is set in Edwardian London. It comes at a point in the musical where the main character, the cockney flower girl Eliza Doolittle, has just been taught how to speak 'like a lady' by the professor Henry Higgins. The song expresses her excitement, while Higgins' housekeeper and servants try to persuade her to go to bed.

Listen out for:

- The **32-bar song form** of each chorus: **A** at 0:20, **A** at 0:32, **B** at 0:45, **A** at 0:56.
- The **light, dance-like orchestral accompaniment**, with prominent parts for **woodwind, glockenspiel, strings** and **pizzicato cellos and bass** – combined with the melody line, this helps to convey Eliza's feelings of happiness.
- The **clearly pronounced words** reflecting Eliza's newfound ability to 'speak like a lady'.
- The three **tenuto chords** that occur at the start of the fourth phrase in each chorus, and the **rubato** used elsewhere.
- The use of **brass** and **timpani** to **reinforce** the endings of each verse.
- The use of **spoken dialogue** in between each chorus, as the housekeeper and servants tell Eliza to go to bed.
- The **countermelody** in the second chorus, sung by the housekeeper and servants. Notice how this is sung while the soloist holds on to longer notes, so that the words of both lines can be clearly heard.

TEST YOURSELF

1. What is 32-bar song form?
2. What type of ensemble usually accompanies the singers in a musical?
3. How does the style of singing in music theatre differ from that of opera?
4. What is rubato, and why do singers in a musical use it?

Film music

The first films were **silent**, and to create more of an atmosphere for the audience, a **live pianist, organist** or **small orchestra** played music to complement the action. The advent of the **talkies** in **1927** allowed a **recorded soundtrack** to be added to a film. Rather than make do with existing pieces, directors started to use **specially composed scores**, often written for **full orchestra** by **European-born classical composers** such as Erich Korngold and Max Steiner. They brought with them their knowledge of **programme music, operatic techniques** and **dazzling orchestration**, producing lavish and sophisticated orchestral scores of the sort that you can still hear today in the music of John Williams.

As film has developed, so have many different approaches to writing soundtracks. Today you can find soundtracks in all sorts of **jazz, popular and classical music styles**.

Three famous contemporary film composers and a few of their films are:

- **John Williams** (*Star Wars, Harry Potter* and *Indiana Jones*)
- **Hans Zimmer** (*Pirates of the Caribbean* and *The Simpsons Movie*)
- **Thomas Newman** (*WALL-E, American Beauty* and *Erin Brokovich*).

FEATURES TO LISTEN OUT FOR

You might come across musical ideas that are intended to convey:

- A **mood or emotion** (such as love, sadness, fear or excitement)
- Someone's **character** (establishing them as evil, kind, funny, strong, etc.)
- An **event** (such as a race, battle or storm)
- A general **atmosphere** (such as birdsong-like music for a scene set in the country, military-sounding music for an army waiting to attack, or a waltz for a scene set in a ballroom)
- A certain **place** (for instance, using the French national anthem for a scene set in Paris)
- A particular **time in history** (such as Baroque music for the 17th century).

Main characters often have their own **separate musical themes**. The musical **arrangement** of the theme is often **changed** to depict what the character is **feeling** or **experiencing**. One famous example is Darth Vader's theme in the *Star Wars* films, which can be heard whenever the villain Darth Vader enters on screen.

◠ Watch and listen to...

'VERTIGO OPENING SCENE – ROOFTOP CHASE' ON YOUTUBE

This clip on YouTube is from the start of a film called *Vertigo*, with music by **Bernard Hermann**. Bernard Hermann is an important film composer who collaborated with the director Alfred Hitchcock many times. The music in this scene plays an important part in establishing the main character's **fear of heights**. The scene depicts a criminal being chased across some rooftops by a policeman and a detective. The detective slips and ends up holding on to a gutter by his fingertips. The policeman tries to rescue him, but slips and plunges to his death.

Listen out for the **threatening mood** and **excitement** of the opening chase, which is created musically by:

- The **frenetic, chromatic figure** in the **strings** that opens the sequence, which is used as an **ostinato**
- The **dissonant harmonies** and **extensive use of chromaticism**
- The **jagged leaps** in the **brass** (creating a **disjunct** melody)
- The use of **low register instruments** such as the **bass clarinet**.

When the detective looks down for the first time as he hangs from the gutter, his sense of **panic** is conveyed musically by:

- A **loud, dissonant chord**, played by **brass and wind** in a **higher register** – this provides a strong contrast with the low-register music from before
- Use of **swirling harp glissandi**.

When the policeman falls, the **low brass notes** that were first heard when the detective slipped down the roof are **repeated** and used to bring the scene to an end on a **low held note**. This helps to convey the finality of the policeman's death.

TEST YOURSELF

1. What type of ensemble are most film scores written for?
2. How might a main character in a film be represented musically?
3. Name **three** different types of idea (such as a sense of place) that film music can be used to communicate.

World music

Music of the Caribbean

The Caribbean is made up of thousands of islands, the largest of which include Cuba and Jamaica, that lie between **North and South America**. Many different genres of music have developed in the region, such as ska, punta, reggae, soca, calypso and son. You won't be expected to know about any of these genres in great detail, but you should **listen** to enough Caribbean music to be able to distinguish it from African and Indian music.

KEY FEATURES

A few very general characteristics of Caribbean music are:

- **Syncopated** and **repetitive** rhythms
- **Major keys** and **simple, diatonic harmonies**
- **English** or **Spanish lyrics**
- **Call and response** between a **soloist** and **backing chorus**
- The use of **parallel movement**.

Unusual instruments that you might not have come across before include:

- **Latin American percussion** such as the **congas** (a pair of tall drums which are played with the hands) and the **guiro** (a type of gourd that is scraped with a stick)
- The **tres** (a **Cuban guitar** used in **son**)
- **Steel pans** (a **metal pan** that is dented inside to produce a series of different notes, used in **Carnival** music).

Other instruments frequently used are the **guitar**, **trumpet**, **piano** and **violin**.

Some Caribbean music has a **laid-back, relaxed** feel (such as **reggae** and **calypso**), while other styles are more **up-tempo** and perfect for **dancing** (such as **son** and **merengue**). We'll look at these four genres in a bit more detail.

REGGAE

Reggae is a type of **popular music** from **Jamaica** which developed during the late **1960s**, and is particularly associated with the **Rastafarian** movement. It shows influences of **traditional African music** and **American genres** such as **jazz** and **rhythm and blues**.

🎧 Listen to...

'IS THIS LOVE?' BY BOB MARLEY

Characteristic features include:

- The **Jamaican dialect** of the singer
- The **laid-back**, **steady tempo** and $\frac{4}{4}$ metre
- The **staccato organ chords** on the **backbeats** (played on a type of electronic organ known as a **Hammond organ**, which is often used in reggae music)
- **Simple, diatonic harmonies** based around chords **I, IV and V**
- The use of **backing singers** in the chorus
- A **repeated riff** played on **bass guitar**
- **Brass countermelodies** towards the end of the song, from 3:11 onwards (a **horn section** frequently appears in reggae).

CALYPSO

Calypso comes from the island of **Trinidad** and is particularly associated with the festival of **Carnival**. Its origins lie in the music of the **African slaves** who were imported to work on the sugar plantations. Calypso singers vie with one another to come up with the most **inventive, controversial and witty lyrics**, which often make fun of politicians or reflect current issues.

🎧 Listen to...

'STELLA' BY MIGHTY SPARROW

Characteristic features include:

- The **major key** and **simple, diatonic harmonies**
- The $\frac{2}{4}$ metre
- A lot of **syncopation** in the **repetitive** melody
- The use of **brass instruments** which move in **parallel motion**
- The **simple structure**: an instrumental break, verse and chorus x4
- **Candid lyrics** that tell about Mighty Sparrow's relationship with his girlfriend Stella.

SON

Son is a style of music from **Cuba** that mixes **Spanish** and **African** influences, and is a predecessor of the modern dance style **salsa**. It was particularly popular in the **1920s–40s**, and although **traditional son** has since become quite unfashionable in Cuba, the hugely successful album *Buena Vista Social Club* has endeared this style to a worldwide audience.

∩ Listen to...

'BRUCA MANIGUÁ' BY IBRAHIM FERRER

Ibrahim Ferrer was a member of the famous *Buena Vista Social Club* and recorded this song at the age of 71.

Most son pieces are split into **two halves**: a **slow first section** and a **faster second section** (which is known as the montuno). Characteristic features of each can be found in this song.

The first section has:

- A **laid-back melody** that is passed between **violin** and **trumpet** before the **voice** enters
- A **repetitive bass riff**
- A **pianist filling out the harmony** with **staccato chords** and **short runs**
- **Trumpet fills** in **parallel 3rds** (e.g. at 0:41).

The second section, which begins at 2:28, is **faster** and more **syncopated**. It features:

- **Call and response** between a **soloist** and **chorus**, where the soloist **improvises short phrases** and the chorus **responds in harmony**
- **Improvised solos** on the violin and trumpet.

Listen out as well for the **slow harmonic rhythm**, the $\frac{4}{4}$ **metre**, the **Spanish lyrics**, the **parallel movement** in the piano and trumpet parts, and the use of **Latin American percussion**. All of these features can be found in most son music.

MERENGUE

Merengue is a style of popular music from the **Dominican Republic** that developed in the **1920s**. It is **fast** and **energetic**, and designed for **dancing**.

🎧 Listen to...

'EN TUS MANOS' BY MILLY QUEZADA

Characteristic features include:

- The **fast tempo** and $\frac{2}{4}$ **metre**
- The **quick, syncopated pattern** in the **piano**
- The **trumpet interjections** (often in **parallel 3rds**)
- The **Spanish lyrics**
- The **call and response** in the **chorus** between the **soloist** and a **group of backing singers**
- The use of **Latin American percussion** such as the **congas**.

TEST YOURSELF

1. Describe **two** musical characteristics of reggae.
2. Name **two** types of Latin American percussion found in Caribbean music.
3. What happens in the second section (the montuno) of a son piece?

Music of Africa

Africa is a huge continent that contains many diverse styles of music, and trying to learn about them all would be impossible. Instead you should aim to get an overall feel for the characteristics of African music, rather than any in-depth knowledge. Make sure you can identify what makes it sound different to Caribbean and Indian music. The best way to do this is to **listen** to a variety of African music – a number of suggestions are given below.

KEY FEATURES

African music often displays the following general characteristics:

RHYTHM, METRE AND TEMPO

- Rhythms can sometimes be very **complicated** but tend to form **repetitive patterns** that have a **strong rhythmic drive** – **ostinatos** are common.
- **Syncopation** features in much African music.
- The use of **polyrhythm** is common in percussion music, in which conflicting rhythm patterns are heard at the same time.
- African music frequently has a **lively tempo**.

HARMONY AND TONALITY

- **Major keys** are common.
- Harmonies are usually quite **simple** – many songs are based on the **repetition of a few chords** (such as I, IV and V).
- Modulation is **rare**.
- Instrumental music is often **modal**. For example, the kora is usually tuned to the Lydian mode and the mbira to the Mixolydian mode.

MELODY AND TEXTURE

- Melodies are often built on **short**, **repeated** phrases and based on **pentatonic** or **hexatonic** scales.
- They usually have an **improvisatory feel**.
- **Call and response** phrases are often used – these usually occur between a **soloist** (who sings or plays a phrase) and a **larger group** that responds with an answering phrase.
- Many pieces have a **melody and accompaniment** texture, although more **complex**, **layered** textures are often built up in instrumental music.

STRUCTURE AND FORM

- Many instrumental pieces are based on a repeated **ostinato**.
- Songs frequently have a **verse-chorus** structure.
- There may be a **freer, improvised section** at the beginning of a piece before the main melody begins.

NORTH AFRICA

North African music sounds quite different to South African music as it has a distinct **Arabic** flavour. This means that melodies often have a **modal** feel, a **narrow range** and use a lot of **ornamentation**.

Three typical instruments are:

1. The **doumbek**, a type of **drum**
2. The **oud**, a type of **lute**
3. The **zurna**, a **reed instrument** similar to the oboe, with a piercing, nasal sound.

∩ Listen to...

'DIDI' BY KHALED

Khaled is a very successful singer from Alegria. This song is an example of **raï**, a popular style of Alegrian music that combines European, African and Arabic influences.

- ■ The song begins with a section for **unturned percussion** that sounds typically **African**
- ■ A **zurna** then enters with the melody
- ■ The singer enters with a vocal line that feels very **Arabic** due to its **narrow range**, **quick rhythms**, **melismas** and **ornamentation**
- ■ A **bass guitar** and **drum kit** are added, displaying the **Western** influences.

WEST AND EAST AFRICA

West and East African music encompasses a whole range of styles, from **traditional call-and-response songs** and **complex, layered percussion music** to a thriving **pop scene** in the cities. Popular instruments in these regions include:

1. The **kora**, which is like a cross between a harp and lute, with a **large gourd** and **long neck** that supports **21 strings**
2. The **balafon**, a type of large **xylophone**
3. The **mbira**, an instrument made up of small metal keys fixed to a wooden board – sometimes known as a **thumb piano**
4. **Drums** such as the **djembe** and **talking drum**.

The music played by all of these instruments is usually based around repetitive **ostinatos**, with a strong rhythmic drive and a steady pulse.

∩ Listen to...

'SALAMAN' BY TOUMANI DIABATÉ AND BALLAKÉ SISSOKO

Diabaté and Sissoko are two famous kora players from Mali in West Africa.

Characteristic features include:

- ■ A **free**, almost **unaccompanied introduction** that leads into the main theme
- ■ A 4-bar accompaniment pattern that repeats continuously to form an **ostinato**
- ■ A **major key** and very **simple harmony** – the piece basically alternates between two different chords

- Use of **syncopation**, both in the bass line and melody
- A melody made up of **short, improvised phrases** with **ornaments** and **quick runs**.

'CHEMUTENGURE' BY THOMAS MAPFUMO

Thomas Mapfumo is a musician from Zimbabwe in East Africa, whose political songs and anti-government stance led to his exile from the country.

Characteristic features include:

- The **upbeat** feel to the song
- The **major key** and **simple harmony**, with the repetition of chords **I, IV and V**
- The **improvisatory** feel to the vocal line, which is very **repetitive** and made up of **short, falling phrases**
- Use of the **mbira**, which starts the song and keeps up a repetitive **ostinato** throughout
- The breathy flutes moving in **parallel**, repeating the same **riff** throughout
- The **short, homophonic** phrases sung by the backing singers.

SOUTH AFRICA

Christian missionaries have played a part in shaping South African music, and the influence of the church in this area has led to the prominence of gospel music and other types of **a cappella** singing.

⌒ Listen to...

'HOMELESS' BY LADYSMITH BLACK MAMBAZO

Ladysmith Black Mambazo is a hugely successful a cappella group that sings in a traditional Zulu style.

Characteristic features include:

- The division of voices into a **soloist** and **chorus**
- The **call and response** textures
- The **unusual vocal effects** used
- The **simple harmonies** and **repetitive** melody
- The **homophonic** texture of the chorus
- The **syncopations** that arise in part from the **natural rhythms** of the words.

Indian music

India has a whole range of musical styles, from folk to classical and popular music. Over recent decades the Bollywood film industry has thrived and many singers have gained considerable recognition through this medium. However, the most established musical tradition is **Indian classical music**.

Indian classical music has a long history of around 3000 years (dating back to 1700 BC). The music is learned by ear and performed from memory – typically, a student will undergo a type of apprenticeship with a highly regarded performer, which is known as a **master-student tradition**.

INSTRUMENTS

The instruments you are most likely to come across are:

- **Sitar**: a type of plucked string instrument with frets, a very long neck and over 20 strings. Only seven of these are used to play the melody – the others vibrate to create a distinctive shimmering sound.
- **Sarod**: similar to the sitar, except that this instrument has no frets, which allows the player to slide between notes – listen out for lots of **glissandos**.
- **Sarangi**: a **bowed** string instrument.
- **Bansuri**: a bamboo **flute**.
- **Tanpura**: a plucked instrument with four strings, used to play the **drone**.
- **Tabla**: a pair of small **drums**.

Indian classical music usually consists of three elements: a **melody line**, a **rhythmic pattern** and a **drone**.

MELODY

The melody is based on a scale of notes called a **raga**.

There are **many different** ragas, and most of them are associated with a particular **time of day**, **season** or **mood**. Usually the **ascending pattern** of the scale will be **slightly different** to the **descending one** (like the western melodic minor scale). Some notes in each raga will also be **more important** than others, and will be **emphasised** in the music.

Before a performance everyone will **agree which raga to use**, and the sitar player (for example) will then **improvise a melody** around the **notes of the raga**. To begin with, they will explore the notes of the raga in quite a **simple, laid-back way**, but as the piece progresses the improvisation will become **more and more complex**.

You are likely to hear the following techniques in the melody:

- **Pitch bends** – a slide up or down to a note (the note is 'bent')
- **Glissandos** between different notes
- **Rapid scales**
- **Ornamentation**
- **Dialogue** with the tabla player, as the sitar **imitates** rhythms played by the tabla.

RHYTHM

Each piece is based on a **cycle of beats** called a **tala**. There are a range of different talas, each with a **set number of beats**, some of which will be **accented**. One of the most common talas is tintal, a cycle of 16 beats (similar to four bars of $\frac{4}{4}$).

The tabla player **improvises rhythms** around the tala, which gradually become **more complex** as the piece progresses.

DRONE

There is no real harmony in Indian classical music – instead a **drone** is played throughout a piece by the **tanpura**. It is based on the **most important note(s)** in the raga.

STRUCTURE

Most pieces have **three main sections**:

Alap (free, slow, no tabla)	Gat (tabla enters)	Jhalla (becomes faster)

- The alap is a **slow, improvised introduction** in **free time**. The melody instrument **introduces and explores the notes of the raga**, accompanied only by the **drone**.
- The **tabla** enters in the gat, creating a clear sense of pulse. This section is often based on a **pre-composed idea**, which the melody instrument uses as a basis for **improvisation**. The music **builds in excitement** as the final section is approached.
- The improvisation in the jhalla becomes **faster** and more **virtuosic**, with cascades of scales and intricate rhythms.

⌒ Listen to...

'RAGA DEVGIRI BILAWAL' BY RAVI SHANKAR AND ALLA RAKHA

Ravi Shankar is one of the most famous **sitar** players, and **Alla Rakha** often accompanies him on **tabla**.

Listen out for:

- The **drone**, which can be heard on its own at the very start – the **sitar** enters shortly after with a descending scale.
- The **free, improvisatory** feel to the **alap**.
- The entry of the **tabla** at 1:38 – this is the beginning of the **gat**. Notice how the sitar part becomes much more **rhythmic** at this point.
- The many **pitch bends** and **rapid scales** in the sitar part.
- The gradual **build up** to a fast, exciting climax.

TEST YOURSELF

1. Name **two** melody instruments found in Indian classical music.
2. What is the correct term for the held or repeated note(s) that last throughout a piece?
3. Name **three** techniques or features that might be used by the melody instrument when improvising.
4. What is the pair of small Indian drums called?

Glossary

Accent. Emphasis on a note or chord (sometimes indicated by the symbol >).

Acciaccatura. A very short ornamental note played just before a principal melodic note.

Alto. A low female voice.

Appoggiatura. An ornamental note that falls on the beat as a dissonance and then resolves by step onto the main note.

Arpeggio. A chord in which the notes are played one after the other rather than at the same time.

Backbeat. In pop music this refers to accenting beats 2 and 4 in $\frac{4}{4}$ time.

Baritone. A male voice that lies between tenor and bass.

Bass. (1) The lowest male voice. (2) The lowest-pitched line in a piece of music, on which the harmonies are based.

Beat. The beat in a piece of music is a regular pulse that we can clap along to. The number of beats in each bar is indicated by the **time signature**.

Binary form. A musical structure of two sections with contrasting material in each (AB).

Blue note. A note (usually the third, fifth or seventh degree of a major scale) performed at a slightly lower pitch than normal for expressive effect.

Bridge. In jazz and pop music, a contrasting passage that connects two longer sections.

Broken chord. A chord in which the notes are played one after the other rather than at the same time.

Cadence. Formed by the last two chords of a phrase, a type of musical punctuation.

Call and response. A pair of phrases, performed by different musicians, in which the second phrase is heard as a reply to the first. This term normally refers to jazz, pop and world music.

Chimes. A percussion instrument consisting of a row of metal tubes, tuned to different notes, which are struck with a hammer.

Chorus. (1) The repeated refrain in a verse-chorus structure. (2) A movement for whole choir in a large-scale choral work. (3) A small choir. (4) A digital effect that thickens the sound by superimposing similar versions of the same track.

Chromatic. Notes that don't belong to the scale of the key the music is currently in. For example, B♮ and D♯ are chromatic notes in the key of F major. Opposite of **diatonic**.

Coda. A section of music that ends a piece.

Compound time. A metre in which the main beat is sub-divided into three equal portions (e.g. a dotted-crotchet beat divided into three quavers). Opposite of **simple time**.

Consonance. Notes that are consonant sound pleasing when played together. Opposite of **dissonance**.

Continuo. An accompanying part in instrumental music of the Baroque period. The continuo is played by a bass instrument (such as cello) and a harmony instrument (such as harpsichord).

Contrapuntal. Adjective to describe music that uses **counterpoint**.

Countermelody. A second melody in a piece that is heard at the same time as the main melody, to provide contrast.

Counterpoint. A texture in which two or more melodic lines, each one significant in itself, are played together at the same time.

Crescendo. A gradual increase in dynamic.

Cross rhythm. The presence in a passage of music of conflicting rhythms (e.g. groups of three notes played in one line while groups of two are played simultaneously in another).

Dialogue. When two or more instruments or voices have a musical 'conversation', with the individual parts responding to one another with different ideas and phrases.

Diatonic. Notes that belong to the scale of the key the music is currently in. For example, B♭ and D are diatonic notes in the key of F major. Opposite of **chromatic**.

Disjunct. A disjunct melody moves by leaps, or intervals larger than a 2nd.

Dissonance. Notes that are dissonant produce a clashing sound when played together. Opposite of **consonance**.

Distortion. A digital effect that alters the sound of an instrument so that it becomes rougher and harsher.

Dominant. The fifth note of a scale. For example, C is the dominant of F.

Dotted rhythm. A rhythm that contains pairs of notes in the pattern long–short. The first note is dotted and the second is a third of the dotted note's value (e.g. dotted crotchet–quaver).

Double stopping. Playing two notes at once on a bowed string instrument.

Doubling. A note or passage in one part is played by another part at the same time, either at the same **pitch** or at a different **octave**.

Drum machine. An electronic device that replicates the sounds of various percussion instruments.

Dynamics. How loudly or softly the music is played; the volume of the music.

Ensemble. A group of musicians performing together.

Falsetto. A vocal technique used by men to sing notes higher than those within their normal voice range.

Fill. A short passage of music between two sections of a melody.

Free time. Describes music without a regular pulse.

Funk. A type of popular music that developed in the 1960s, combining soul, jazz and R 'n' B.

Glissando. A slide between two notes.

Hammond organ. An electronic organ invented in the 1930s.

Harpsichord. The most common keyboard instrument of the Baroque period. Similar to the piano, except that the strings are plucked rather than hit.

Hexatonic scale. A scale made up of six notes.

Homophony. A texture in which one part has the melody and the other parts accompany.

Horn section. In popular music, a group of wind and brass players (frequently made up of trumpets, trombones and saxophones).

Imitation. A melodic idea in one part is immediately copied by another part, often at a different pitch, while the first part continues with other music.

Interval. The distance between two notes. For example, the interval between the notes F and A is a 3rd (A is the third note of the F major scale).

Key. The key indicates the scale that a section or piece of music is based on. For example, music in the key of G major uses notes of the G major scale.

Layered. A texture made up of independent lines which are designed to be heard together.

Loop. A short segment of music that is repeated a number of times in succession.

Major and minor. Describe different types of intervals, chords, keys and scales. Minor intervals are smaller than major intervals by a semitone (e.g. F to A is a major 3rd, whereas F to A♭ is a minor 3rd. A major chord, key or scale contains a major third above the tonic, whereas a minor chord, scale or key contains a minor third (e.g. a D major chord contains the notes D–F♯–A, while a D minor chord uses the notes D–F♮–A).

Melody and accompaniment. A texture in which one part has the melody while the other parts accompany.

Metre. The metre refers to the pulse of the music and is indicated by the **time signature**.

Metronome mark. An indication of how fast to play a piece by specifying how many beats per minute there should be. E.g. a metronome mark of ♩ = 60 means that there are 60 crotchet beats per minute, or one crotchet beat per second.

Minuet and trio. A movement in ABA form. The minuet (A) is an elegant dance in ¾, while the trio (B) provides contrasting material.

Mode. Different types of seven-note scales, other than the major and minor.

Modulation. (1) The process of changing key in a passage osf music.

Mute. A device that can be fitted to an instrument to quieten the sound.

Octave. An interval formed from two notes that are 12 semitones apart. Both notes have the same name.

Opera. A dramatic work in which the words are sung rather than spoken. Unlike the musical, the opera is classical in style.

Ornament. Small musical additions that decorate a melody. See **acciaccatura**, **appoggiatura** and **trill**.

Ostinato. A repeating melodic, harmonic or rhythmic motif, heard continuously throughout part or the whole of a piece.

Overdubbing. Recording a new part over the top of existing material.

Parallel motion. Movement of two or more parts in the same direction, with the interval between them remaining essentially the same.

Pedal note. A sustained or continuously repeated pitch, often in the bass, that is heard against changing harmonies.

Phrase. A short musical unit, similar to a phrase or a sentence in speech.

Piccolo. A small flute that sounds an octave higher than written.

Pitch bend. A short slide up or down to a main note.

Pizzicato. A direction to pluck notes on a string instrument.

Polyphony. A texture in which two or more melodic lines, each one significant in itself, are played together at the same time.

Pulse. A regularly recurring sense of **beat** common to most styles of music.

Range. The notes that a singer or instrumentalist can sing or play.

Rapping. Speaking rhythmically (often with rhyme) to a beat.

Rastafarian. A religious movement that developed in the 1930s in Jamaica.

Register. A part of the **range** of an instrument or voice.

Relative major, relative minor. Keys that have the same **key signature** but a different **tonic**. The tonic of a relative minor is three semitones below the tonic of its relative major (e.g. C major and A minor).

Rhythm and blues. A harder-edged form of blues which emerged in American cities in the 1940s.

Riff. A short, catchy melodic or rhythmic idea that is repeated throughout a jazz or pop song.

Rock and roll. A genre of popular music that developed in the USA during the 1940s and 50s.

Rondo. A musical structure in which a main melody alternates with contrasting sections (ABACADA).

Root. The note on which a chord is built and after which it takes its name. For example, the root of a chord of D minor is the note D.

Rubato. Slight changes to the tempo of a performance – speeding up or slowing down to make the music more expressive.

Sample. A short section from a recorded audio track that can be digitally manipulated and altered for insertion into a new track.

Sampler. An electronic device, like a synthesiser, that allows the user to alter and manipulate musical **samples**.

Scale. A sequence of notes that move by step either upwards or downwards. Different types of scales have different patterns of **intervals**.

Scherzo and trio. A movement in ABA form. The scherzo (A) is a lively dance in $\frac{3}{4}$, while the trio (B) provides contrasting material.

Semitone. Half of a tone. The smallest interval in Western music in general use.

Sequence. Immediate repetition of a melodic or harmonic idea at a different pitch, or a succession of different pitches.

Seventh chord. A chord made up of a triad and a note a 7th above the root.

Simple time. A metre in which the main beat is sub-divided into two equal portions (e.g. a crotchet beat divided into two quavers). Opposite of **compound time**.

Soprano. The highest female voice.

Soul. A genre of popular music that developed in the USA in the late 1950s, combining elements from gospel with rhythm and blues.

Staccato. Detached. Refers to notes that are held for less time than their value indicates, so they are shortened and separated from each other.

Strophic. A type of song in which the same music is used for each verse of the lyrics. Opposite of **through-composed**.

Subdominant. The fourth degree of a diatonic scale.

Syncopation. Placing the accents in parts of the bar that are not normally emphasised, such as on weak beats or between beats.

Tempo. The speed of the music.

Tenor. A high male voice.

Tenuto. An articulation mark that indicates a note should be emphasised, either by playing it slightly louder or holding it for longer.

Ternary form. A musical structure of three sections. The outer sections are similar and the central one contrasting (ABA).

Texture. The relationship between the various simultaneous lines in a passage of music, dependent on such features as the number and function of the parts and the spacing between them.

Through-composed. A type of song in which different music is used for each verse of the lyrics. Opposite of **strophic**.

Time signature. Two numbers (for example $\frac{2}{4}$ or $\frac{6}{8}$) at the start of a stave that indicate the metre of the music. The bottom number indicates the type of beat (such as crotchet or quaver) and the top number shows how many of those beats are in each bar.

Timpani. Also known as kettledrums, these are the large drums in the percussion section of an orchestra, each tuned to a different bass note.

Tone. (1) An interval of two semitones; a major second. (2) The quality of sound (or timbre) of an instrument or voice.

Tonic. The starting note of a major or minor scale, and the note from which a key takes its name. E.g. F is the tonic of F major.

Triad. A chord of three notes: a bass note and notes a 3rd and 5th above it.

Trill. An ornament consisting of a rapid alternation of two adjacent pitches.

Triplet. A group of three equal notes played in the time normally taken by two of the same type.

Tritone. An interval of six semitones.

Unison. Simultaneous performance of the same pitch or pitches by more than one person.

Variation form. A musical structure in which the main theme is varied a number of times.

Verse. A section in a song that usually has lyrics unique to that section (they tend to change for each verse).

Verse-chorus form. A type of popular song in which, in its most basic structure, the **verses** are interspersed with a repeated **chorus**.

Vibrato. A performing technique in which the pitch of a note wavers rapidly.

Virtuoso. A highly-skilled singer or instrumentalist, capable of performing technically difficult music.